# P E A C E
## POWER UP YOUR LIFE

**SANDRA AND DANIEL BISKIND**

**First in the CODEBREAKER PLATINUM Series**

**PEACE: Power Up Your Life**
**First in the CODEBREAKER PLATINUM series**
Version 1.1

Published by EMISSARY COMMUNICATIONS LLC

ISBN: 978-1-941142-61-5

CAUTION: SPIRITUALLY INTOXICATING!

Do not drive or operate heavy machinery while under the influence of this book.

# ACCLAIM FOR SANDRA AND DANIEL BISKIND

**JACK CANFIELD -** Co-author of *Chicken Soup for the Soul* series, *The Success Principles* and a featured teacher in *The Secret*
Sandra and Daniel are profound healers, trainers, speakers and authors who do some exceptional transformational work. I've experienced their work and found it truly life changing — so much so that I had them work with my entire staff with magical results. They have an amazing ability to shift energy and remove blocks on very deep levels.

From the first time I sat down with them I knew something special and profound was about to happen. Their unconditional love, joy and radiance fills the room. An hour later I left more calm, more centered, more my true self and more creative than I can remember. They are the real deal and I highly recommend them and their work. It is transformational wizardry at its best.

**WILLIAM BRYANT -** Former Chairman of the Board, American Chamber of Commerce Executives

Thank you beyond words for conceiving and writing *"PEACE: Power Up Your Life,"* the first book in your CODEBREAKER PLATINUM Series.

Some years ago I was the President and CEO of the largest metropolitan Chamber of Commerce in the United States. If I would have had this publication at that time, our transformation work would have been more efficient, and for sure, more peaceful. Count on this: the first thing I would have done would have been to furnish copies of *"PEACE"* to my Board of Directors, our entire staff and to all my family members. Simply fantastic! If the next book in your series is just half as enlightening, I may just un-retire.

**DEREK RYDAL -** Transformational coach, best-selling author, creator of *The Law of Emergence*

"I've worked with a lot of healers, but rarely do I meet one who is as quick to the heart of the matter as Sandra. In a matter of minutes, she was tuned into the core issues I was dealing with and the root causes, and a few minutes later I could feel a tangible shift, like a weight had been lifted and a new level of energy had been opened. Something was palpably different about me — and all of this in minutes - not months! I look forward to what's possible with her incredible work, and encourage anyone struggling with issues (especially the seemingly unsolvable ones) to experience this for themselves."

**GARY RUSH -** Anthony Robbins Business and Success Coach,

For all my life I have been uncomfortable expressing love to the people closest to me. There has always been this resistance to express the one emotion that is the essence of our existence.

As a result, there has always been this hole in my life that I ignored and that has denied me the depth and richness of life I deserve. Sandra, in just three sessions, nailed what had happened in my past and knew what was preventing me from being the person I so desperately wanted to be. She has a rare gift and talent to pick up what the blocks are and how to resolve them. As a coach for Tony Robbins and with many mentors in personal development, I know for a fact that very few have this ability.

After working with her I feel more at peace with myself and know that I am now on track to express and experience more love in my life.

**ALISON HORA -** Professional Dive Instructor

To sift through my thoughts and find a completely different person than two days ago has brought me to a place of great appreciation and Sandra I need to thank you for this. For me the amazement of your work, is that my life's structure is still there, people didn't disappear. But, my deep emotions have changed. The shift that has taken place within me is unbelievable.

If I was asked two days ago if it were possible to be clear and free from such deep inner pain and confusion so quickly, my answer would have been no. I would not have been able to even imagine my way to this place that I am now at. In the mornings I now wake with excitement for my life. My energy levels have been restored and I am happy and so truly honored to have met you.

**AMBER BRECH-HOLLINS -** Special Events Photographer

One of the most important decisions I have ever made in my life was to work on a personal level with Sandra and Daniel. I have worked with them for more than 8 years because doing this work shifts me from crisis point to a place of absolute relief and neutrality in a matter of minutes.

It has transformed my life on every level and in every part of my life dramatically and continues to do so. Whether it be for me personally with something I'm working on or in my relationships with my husband, children, work colleagues, family & friends or in my businesses, every area is enriched and improved.

I am forever grateful for the peace and joy that it brings me back to. For bringing me back to my true self. My true north. Thank you, Sandra and Daniel.

**ROBERT HURST -** Business Owner and Entrepreneur

To say I am passionate about the new and improved direction in my life would be an understatement. I feel like an i7 processor in a 386 world. I have used Jim Rohn, Tony Robbins, Dennis Waitley and many others over the last 30 years. Nothing I have ever done can compare to the breakthrough technology that I have been lucky enough to experience through Sandra and Daniel and their Ultimate Mind Shift program.

**JAMES HOLLINS -** Business Owner and Entrepreneur

WOW! Words almost can't do justice to the incredible work that Sandra and Daniel do. To be able to go from totally on edge, stressed, depressed, angry, and "over life", to feeling happy, content, aligned, powerful, strong, and "in love" with life again, all in the space of a thirty minute session — Truly amazing! I really appreciate being ME again.

**ALISON QUEDLEY -** Former publisher and editor IN TOUCH magazine

The books in The CODEBREAKER PLATINUM Series are AMAZING just like you both. It comes straight from the heart and is written so deceptively simply. I am sure that people reading it will absorb the words on a very deep level without even realising the changes the words will be making in their lives!! This is a life changing book for anyone who is in any pain and distress, as well as those who want to carry on their journey into the Divine Mind and Love.

Can't wait until I can hold *CODEBREAKER: Discover the Password to Unlock The Best Version Of You* in my hands and feel the power of healing that I know will affect many many souls.

Thank you both for your dedication to humanity and for your ever present loving connection.

# CONTENTS

# INTRODUCTION
# THE CODEBREAKER PLATINUM SERIES

*"When you are connected to your
Divine Mind, you will feel an ocean of
peace and joy moving in you."*

*–Sandra and Daniel Biskind*

The only thing you can be 100% certain of being in your future is yourself.

This book and all the books, programs, and website materials in The CODEBREAKER PLATINUM Series have been conceived and designed to empower you to become the best version of you. Now, more than at any other time in history, there is the emerging potential to make huge shifts in consciousness that can take humanity—and yes, individuals—into a whole new stratosphere of living with peace and love, expanded awareness, confidence, and trust; integrity and empowered neutrality; and mindful oneness with one another and the cosmos.

Collectively, the evolution of our souls is accelerating the realization of the new human: awakened, enlightened, self-actualized and whole. Welcome! This book is dedicated to accelerating your transformation—to supporting your rapid change and profound inner growth.

We are all searching for the same thing. We all want peace, love and joy. We all want to be happy.

An attractive, sixty-year-old American woman, who had never been married and who lived alone with her cat, decided to attend one of our weekend seminars in Los Angeles. She was ever hopeful of finding resolution around an ongoing, emotionally debilitating problem. She was extremely successful in her career and had become a woman of means who had spent 40 years and hundreds of thousands of dollars trying to find peace around an incestuous experience in her teens that continued to torment her and sabotage her life. During a private session after the weekend, we were able to discover the core program that was blocking her from being able to step into her true personal power.

Her emotions around the event were rendered neutral, which enabled her to finally release the negative life pattern ruining her life. In just one session, she shifted from someone who was still traumatized and afraid of never having a fulfilling and meaningful relationship to finally feeling peaceful and optimistic about her future. She was happy.

Happiness often eludes us. Most people are in denial of this truth, which is exactly the way the ego mind likes it. Your ego mind has you seeking pleasure in all the wrong places to alleviate the pain of loneliness and sadness and to distract you from feelings of emptiness and lack of meaning and fulfillment.

Daniel and I both had to overcome many debilitating life challenges where we had to find the inner strength and personal power to thrive in adversity. It was this work that helped us through the tough times and brought us back into alignment with our True Selves. We always kept course correcting back into our hearts where peace was restored.

To experience the richness of life, of real love and authentic forgiveness, we first had to master our minds in order to come to that place of peace. We needed to have gratitude for all we had and all we could give.

Having reached that place inside of ourselves and having assisted thousands of people around the world to do like-wise, we knew the next step in living our life purpose was to write these books. We want to share with you the tools and gifts we have developed over our lifetimes to transform our lives so that you can do the same.

More than encouragement, the books in The CODEBREAKER PLATINUM Series act as guides and mentors on your amazing journey from the head to the heart. For some, this series will provide stimulating new ideas. For others, it will provide confirmation that you are on the right track to everyday enlightenment.

You don't have to change your religious or spiritual beliefs for these books to weave miracles in your life. Remember, you are not alone. To varying degrees, we all face the same chal-lenges. And depending on the software programs you are running in your unique human computer, you will create dif-ferent levels of emotional adjustment as you deal with those challenges.

No matter how daunting or overwhelming your circumstances may seem, just like Daniel and me (along with many others), you can turn your life around.

As you read, absorb, and apply the CODEBREAKER PLATINUM Master Password, you will begin to retrain your mind and transform your emotions and your experience of life. You will accelerate your soul's evolution into enlightenment and wholeness. This will in turn propel you into greater levels of inner peace, joy, happiness, and optimal health—and a closer connection to the divine within you.

# A BRIEF EXPLANATION OF TERMS

Some concepts basic to our work include your True Self, Ego mind programs, Neutrality, The Divine Mind, Living a PLATINUM life and Non-duality.

**YOUR TRUE SELF** is the perfection of who you really are, and peace is an eternal expression of your True Self, which is whole and complete.

**EGO MIND PROGRAMS** are parts of your self image that you've fabricated as opposed to the perfection of your True Self. Say you have an ego mind program that you believe peace can only be experienced fleetingly. You will then create situations that prove that. You can't help but sabotage your career, your relationships, and your health when you believe you can never find lasting peace.

**NEUTRALITY** is a state in which you are free of belief and attachment. Neutrality's open-mindedness enables you to access higher awareness, free of bias, emotion and prejudice. The state of empowered Neutrality is where your ego mind's thoughts and emotions no longer control you. Neutrality is essential to peace and real freedom and is the key to enlightenment.

**THE DIVINE MIND** is the ever-expanding, infinite expression of pure love and joy that expresses itself deep within you when you are no longer held hostage by the ego mind but are free and at peace. It is the source of true reality in contrast to ego mind which is the source of false reality.

**LIVING A PLATINUM LIFE** means you have the skills to remain neutral and empowered regardless of circumstances. A PLATINUM life enables you to live the perfection that you really are free of limiting beliefs and ideas—free of inner turmoil.

Your relationships become more stable; you feel happier and healthier; more vital and creative. With less useless mind chatter, you have a more balanced emotional life. You are in touch with the field of infinite possibilities.

In a PLATINUM life you are continually becoming the best version of you.

**NON-DUALITY** is the natural foundational state of awareness of the unity of subject and object. It is where we understand we are all connected, not only to each other but to our Source and to all life.

*"We need to understand that*

*thoughts are tools.*

*Are we using them as productively*

*as we can?*

*Are our thoughts serving us well,*

*or are we their victims?*

*It's up to us."*

# HOW TO USE THE CODEBREAKER PLATINUM SERIES

*THE WORK: No matter where you are on your own mystical journey into the real world of infinite love, peace, joy and true success you can use these tools and techniques to begin or continue to realign yourself with the high frequencies of the Divine Mind Code.

*FIRST AID: Use *PEACE: Power Up Your Life* as a mentor when you need help on any level. Focus your intention on receiving the guidance you need, open the book randomly, and the chapter or page you see will be what you need to read in that moment. Or, if you prefer, look at the contents page and then read the appropriate section to help you instantly feel better.

*THE DIVINE MIND FIELD: Use this book as a way to attune yourself to the frequency of the Divine Mind Code—accessible through your wholistic consciousness, which incorporates the maximal range of the human mind. The CODE-BREAKER PLATINUM books activate the Master Password so your True Self's attributes of peace, love, awareness, trust, integrity, neutrality, unity and mindfulness are experienced—reconnecting you to your personal power.

*POEMS: When a poem appears, take a deep breath and relax. Do not rush through it, but savor it. Each one has been deliberately chosen to catapult you into your heart and illuminate your soul, flicking the switch on the light within. Join these high frequency beings as they bare their God-drenched souls as often as you can.

**\*MEDITATIONS AND VISUALIZATIONS**: Simple meditations will focus you onto the frequency of the relevant quality in each chapter. Repeating them will also help create new neural pathways in the brain. Eventually these pathways become the dominant thought processing pathways that help raise your level of awareness. Download your free CODEBREAKER PLATINUM meditations at www.TheBiskinds.com.

**\*THE TOOL KIT**: Simple three point "keys" give you a fast and easy way to receive and assimilate information. Read and contemplate them REPEATEDLY until they become like short passwords themselves. They will simply and effectively unlock your life code to access your personal power.

**\*REPROGRAMMING THE BRAIN**: Training the brain via repetition is also an essential way for you to learn. As you create new habit fields in the mind, they become reflected as new neural pathways that change the way the brain functions.

**The teachings will be repeated in short stories, metaphors and analogies going over the same points in different contexts. Override your ego mind's voice when it tells you, "I have heard it all before."**

As one of my teachers in Australia said, "Because I love you so much, I will continue to give you the same information until you are living it."

To maximize its transformational effect in your life, it is important to not only read this book often but to immerse yourself in it—using the practices daily.

# MAP OF AWARENESS

Daniel and I have long been considered experts in the art and science of personal transformation. We have helped thousands of people around the world, from London and New York to Los Angeles and Australasia. In our ongoing research and development, we discovered the Master Password that unlocks the Divine Mind Code for us. It was a fascinating process that revealed a code of such depth that we missed its power at first.

We took our time, as we are asking you to do. As you begin to work with this secret password, multiple uses will be revealed for each concept. People who have read these books three and four times have said that it became even more useful, insightful, and life-changing the more they read them.

We created a Map of Awareness inspired by the Hawkins scale of consciousness from the book *Power vs. Force: The Hidden Determinants of Human Behavior* by David Hawkins, MD, Ph.D.

The Hawkins scale was two-dimensional, measuring consciousness in a vertical line going from 0 to 1,000 with 0 being the lowest state of consciousness. The majority of people are either 200 or below and are firmly entrenched in ego mind thinking. No one at this level of consciousness would even consider picking up, let alone reading, *CODEBREAKER: Discover the Password to Unlock the Best Version of You* or *The CODEBREAKER PLATINUM Series.*

Hawkins calibrated Einstein's consciousness at 499, which he considered the pinnacle of intellect. At 500, your heart opens and you begin to operate out of love. The state of unconditional love begins at 540. Enlightened states calibrate from 600 to 1,000, the theoretical maximum sustainable in a human body. Humanity's greatest masters, including Buddha and Jesus, calibrated at 1,000.

The Integrated Wholeness Scale is three dimensional and logarithmic. It adds a horizontal axis that measures personality issues that need to be resolved as you move from one level of awareness to another. Life challenges can trigger negative emotional responses and all the associated issues. As you move farther along both consciousness and personality sides of the scale together, the way you deal with them becomes more efficient and effective.

Unpacking personality programs from consciousness helps us to understand how high-consciousness people can do otherwise inexplicably low-consciousness deeds.

# The Evolution of the Soul

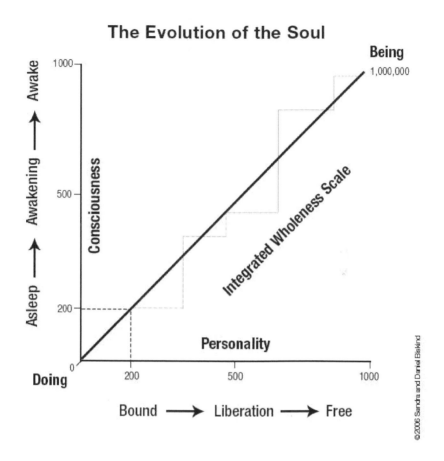

The CODEBREAKER PLATINUM Series presents a life-long process of revelation, mastery, and ongoing practice and training. The immense power and beauty of your True Self is revealed increasingly with every book in the series. The words you are about to read will take you into a place where the mystical world of the Divine Mind guides your life and you are no longer held hostage in the fantasy world of your ego mind. Join us on this inner exploration of the non-dual world that is your True Self.

# THE MASTER PASSWORD

Here is the CODEBREAKER Master Password:

PEACE LOVE AWARENESS TRUST
INTEGRITY NEUTRALITY UNITY MINDFULNESS

PLATINUM is the Master Password that in the correct combination unlocks the secret to the Divine Mind Code for each of us.

This Master Password is like a key that awakens your consciousness and liberates your personality. As Buddha said, "Your mind is everything. What you think you become." You can train your mind, be accountable for your soul choices, attune yourself to the Divine Mind Code and ascend the Integrated Wholeness Scale into enlightened states.

PLATINUM unlocks the code to the inspiring, uplifting, true stories of the heart rather than perpetuating the deceptive, destructive, fictitious stories of the ego mind. This series presents a plan which makes your soul's choice to live by the wisdom of the Divine Mind Code rather than the dictates of the ego mind code a whole lot easier.

You can easily discover the passwords to your ego mind codes, and in doing so reveal the truth that you have been compromised and corrupted by the enemy within—the ego mind.

Some of them go something like this: pathetic, loser, asshole, terrorist, intolerant, negative, unforgivable, malicious.

These words are below 100 on both the consciousness axis and personality axis of the Integrated Wholeness Scale.

**PLATINUM acknowledges you are already perfect and you are much more than the mere sum of your automated programs, conditioned thinking and mindless self-talk. And, as you so well know, you are much more than what your physical senses reveal.**

**You are a PLATINUM being. This is your True Self. Most people never realize this because their soul is asleep. They sleepwalk through life. Activating the PLATINUM password awakens your soul to choose wholeness again.**

**Learn to use the password to decode your life and break through to great loving relationships, real strength and vitality, and the work and financial success you deserve.**

**Make the commitment to start living your PLATINUM life today.**

As you read, absorb, and implement these concepts you will retrain your mind, which transforms your experience of life. Accelerate your soul's journey into enlightenment and wholeness and propel yourself into greater levels of joy, inner peace, happiness, better health, and a closer connection to the divine perfection within you.

Uh oh! What do I have to give up to live a PLATINUM life?

Sex, wine, shopping, credit cards...just kidding! Seriously, you will only be giving up your illusions and stories. You won't miss any of the things you have to give up to live a PLATI-NUM life, but you will naturally feel better and your light will shine brighter and you will attract more love in your life. And, you will have loads of fun.

You have no doubt already learned that you can think positively about what you desire until you are blue in the face, but that does not mean those positive thoughts will manifest as changes in your life. Ultimately, your unconscious programs and patterns are running the show. Until those are corrected your ability to manifest your best intentions will continue to be sabotaged by programs hidden in your unconscious mind.

Your life is a masterpiece in the making. Let us help you fulfill your purpose by changing the inner landscape of your life so the outer landscape of your home, your work, and your relationships can reflect the change you want to be and see.

*"When love and skill work together,*
*expect a masterpiece."*

*–John Ruskin*

The CODEBREAKER PLATINUM series presents groundbreaking concepts that will empower you to move into new levels of awareness, which lead to whole new ways of being. The aim of this system is for you to have a complete mind shift. That is why we call the process The Ultimate Mind Shift.

This series has been intentionally designed to attune you to the supercharged frequency of enlightenment. You could feel very high and sometimes the brain may feel heavy because the energy field created as you read these books reconnects you to the enlightenment frequency. Its vibrational field, including the superconscious frequency of higher awareness, extends beyond that of the conscious and unconscious minds. As your brain processes them, you may experience new and different sensations.

Use the CODEBREAKER PLATINUM password to crack the Divine Mind Code and start living the life of your dreams.

As you read through these books, and as you pick up and implement the Key Passwords one at a time, and then put them together, you will create your own version of the extravagantly rich and beautiful life presented to you in this process of enlightenment.

To maximize the transformational impact in your life, it is important to not only read these books often but to immerse yourself in them and to use the tools on a daily basis.

Here is what you will get out of reading *PEACE: Power Up Your Life* and from using the Ultimate Mind Shift teaching and training process:

- Increase your emotional intelligence, identify problematic habitual emotional responses to conflict in your life, and implement a powerful new strategy to resolve them while keeping peace of mind.
- Develop a strong, unwavering relationship with your True Self and an ability to understand and utilize your inner communication when making decisions in your everyday life.
- Receive energy that supports you and helps you love, and feel loved and understood, regardless of conditions in your external world.
- Create new patterns and habits that support your health and well-being.
- Create the deep and lasting relationship of your dreams with your partner or future partner.
- Experience deeper love and connection and better communication with the people in your life.
- Become more energetically attractive and magnetic.
- Discover deeper meaning and purpose in your life.
- Delete old sabotage programs to free you to be more creative.

- Access your real power and strength, and lead through love.
- Silence the chatter of your ego mind, and master your inner critic.
- Strengthen your connection to your spiritual core to live in a calm and balanced place no matter what life throws at you.
- Experience an energetic frequency that regenerates, rejuvenates, strengthens, and renews every cell in your body.
- Access the mystical world of the Divine Mind which automatically brings your body, mind, and soul into higher levels of awareness.
- Mastery of the simple tools that progressively build a deeper and more sustainable connection to the PLATINUM password and the Divine Mind Code.
- A level of happiness that will astonish and delight you.

Have fun! And remember,

**The secret to enlightenment is to lighten up!**

# WHAT IS ENLIGHTENMENT?

Enlightenment is the state in which you are fully connected to your True Self, often characterized by causeless love and limitless joy.

It is the state where you experience the world without projecting judgment.

Enlightenment empowers you to accept the perfection in everyone and love them without reservation or condition.

It is the peaceful, confident experience of life unfiltered by the programs of your ego mind. In enlightenment, the world is simply a mirror of you and the divine energy within you.

Like many people, have you ever thought, "I don't want to be enlightened and live alone high on a mountain top, laughing at the rest of the world?" After a lifetime's desire to know, understand and live an enlightened life, both Daniel and I have discovered that is not what enlightenment is about at all.

> *"It isn't by getting out of the world that we become enlightened, but by getting into the world...by getting so tuned in that we can ride the waves of our existence and never get tossed because we become the waves."*
>
> *–Ken Kesey*

I was fortunate to have spent many years working with an enlightened American spiritual teacher who visited Melbourne a few times a year. I had just taken a seat when I realized the whole auditorium was full of an intense, iridescent purple light. But where was it coming from? I had been putting on stage shows for many years and had used lighting technicians for special effects many times. No matter where I looked I could not find the banks of lights that would have been needed to fill the whole room with this gorgeous wash of colored light.

I asked the person sitting beside me if they knew why our teacher was using purple light and could he see where the light was coming from. He looked at me quizzically and said in an are-you-for-real voice, "What purple light? There's no purple light on the stage, or in the room." Well, there was purple light in the room I was sitting in! In exasperation, I closed my eyes. The same purple light was flooding my internal world.

So that's where it was coming from—inside me! I was the source of light. When asked, the teacher told me the purple light I was seeing was my own spirit. Obviously I could see this light with my physical eyes but who was seeing it when my eyes were closed? It was my soul—the observer—that part of me that can never die and is capable of fully connecting to my True Self. Like my physical eyes, my spiritual eyes were observing and relaying messages to the brain to process.

I had been working with this spiritual master for over six years and in that time had changed the way I lived my life. I was meditating on a daily basis and still working with other amazing healers and teachers to hone my own ability to be the best version of myself.

I realized that I coped with life challenges with more ease and less drama and was capable of being even more creative, more loving, and more forgiving than ever. And, I was totally addicted to the high of enlightenment. Feelings of joy and love would overwhelm me for no reason at all. I would see total strangers and be in love with all of them—no matter what they looked like. If this was an enlightened state, I wanted more.

During a public session with an Indian guru who was visiting Melbourne, a few hundred people were all invited to come to the front of the room for a hug with this enlightened being. I waited in line for over half an hour. (I would have waited even if I was the last person in line and it was a very long line.) When she held me in her arms close to her chest, she just said, "More. More. More." That became my mantra. More love, more joy, more wonder and fulfilment. If this was an enlightenment state and being connected to my Divine Mind I was on the right path.

In the enlightened state, you understand the great mysteries of life, including that the whole of humanity is one wonderful idea from the mind of God which is manifesting in 7 billion unique ways. From an enlightened perspective, you understand humanity has been hoodwinked into believing what the ego mind has told us—that we are separate from everyone else and need to look outside ourselves for the love, joy, success, health, and well-being that we seek.

> *"Enlightenment is your natural state and your thoughts are the only thing stopping you from having the life you want."*
>
> *–Sandra Biskind*

# WHAT IS PEACE?

*Fully connected to the light of your True Self,*
*Peace is your natural state.*

PEACE is the state of harmony and balance, tranquility, and quiet in which the highest good for all is naturally sought. In this state of serenity, you are free from unsettling thoughts and emotions.

Inner peace is the bedrock upon which your development of a PLATINUM life rests.

By disconnecting from your natural state of peace, you open the door to mental, emotional, and physical distress of all kinds. For example, feelings of despair, grief, and panic and a disconnection from those you love, can overpower your life with devastating results.

Continuing on the downward spiral away from your PLATI-NUM life and inner peace can result in sickness, separation, suicidal thoughts, and even death.

# KEYS TO PEACE

To be in a state of peace, you need to be in harmony with the energy frequency of peace. To attune to this frequency consistently, it helps to set the stage for peace in your home and work and is essential to train your mind and create new habits.

Some simple steps to accomplish this:

- On your inner journey into peace, use mindful meditation daily. Become the observer of your thoughts and feelings without comment or judgment. As you do, the odds are that you will discover emotional triggers that need to be corrected so you can be the neutral observer from a place of peace.
- Make your home and work space as harmonious as possible. Use your creativity and intuition to create a stable, peaceful environment to work, play, and love in. For instance, you could have photos of the people and pets you love around you, hang art of beautiful places in nature, or just gorgeous washes of color—anything that makes you feel inspired and at peace. If your rooms are small or dark place, mirrors opposite the windows to reflect the light and create the illusion of space. Every home in which I have ever lived I have painted white, but you could paint your walls your favorite colors and make sure you declutter your floors and benches. Spirit loves beauty in all forms. That is why the more you create beautiful spaces around you, the more peaceful, uplifted, and content you will feel.

- As often as possible find, a place in nature where you can enjoy the beauty and serenity of your surroundings. Take in the splendor of a sunset or sunrise, and allow yourself to feel the joy of being alive in that moment.
- Get your blood flowing and oxygenate your entire system. Exercise as often as you can: walk, run, dance, lift weights, or just tense and relax. Center yourself and connect with your core essence by practicing yoga, tai chi, chi gong or any of the martial arts practices that require you to find the fluidity and power that comes from inner peace.
- Continually use inquiry—like in Rate Your State and The Four Questions—to stay balanced and mindful, to heighten your level of awareness, and to reinforce your inner peace.
- To experience inner peace you need to forgive. Remember, you are only ever forgiving ego mind programs—both your own and others'—that have been accumulated since birth.
- Often, people want forgiveness to be a mutual exchange. It's not! It's unilateral. Forgiveness is intensely personal and it depends on unconditional love.
- Use the creative visualisation from the story "The Playground" found later in this book. Go back in time and truly forgive anyone—including yourself—who has hurt you.
- True inner peace is not dependent on external circumstances. Paradoxically, it is the state in which you can exert the most constructive influence on external circumstances.

Have you ever felt like someone or something was out to get you? Have you or anyone you know ever suffered through times of distress emotionally, mentally or physically only to be told by doctors that there's nothing they can do? They've tried everything and still don't know what is causing the problem. Have you heard people say, "It's all in your head. Try pain management?"

When your soul chooses to live by the ego mind code instead of the Divine Mind Code, you are out of alignment with your True Self, which always results in a lack of inner peace.

# CHICKEN NECK

This is a story about a man called Matthew. It is the perfect example of how your entire life can spiral out of control when you are not connected to your True Self and your natural state of peace.

It also demonstrates how awesome life can be when you discover the truth, get neutral, and stop listening to the stories of the ego mind.

Matthew was in his mid-50s, somewhat overweight, and about 5' 10" tall. He was married with one child and had grown up in Melbourne.

I learned very quickly that he was seeing me after suffering from a severe and painful outbreak of shingles for over eighteen months. After the third doctor he visited had bluntly said that they had exhausted all they could do for him, the doctor told Matthew he should try some form of relaxation. "After all," the doctor said, "it can't hurt."

Matthew was a business man working in a high executive position in a huge Australian company who normally would never consider any alternative form of healing. His tolerance for the excruciating pain, however, was at an all-time low. The torturous pain had worn him down enough that he agreed to try anything, just so long as he could reduce the pain and regain some level of peace—even if that meant trying something as whacky as meditating.

I had come highly recommended, and he agreed to a private session but only after I told him I couldn't help him with the pain if he only wanted to learn meditation. Matthew would have to let me work with him on a deeper level.

He responded by telling me he did not believe in anything like this and did not want any crystals, candles, or that "new age" music. Here was another challenge. He lived over an hour away from my home, so I suggested he find someone closer to where he lived. He insisted that I was the one who had been recommended and I was the one he was going to work with. He was a man who was used to getting what he wanted.

The next day Matthew travelled from Melbourne to the seaside town of Geelong to have his first private session. He sat in his car for more than an hour trying to get calm before he mustered up the courage to come in to learn how to get calm. When he walked into the main room, he became agitated immediately.

Without a word of greeting the first thing out of his mouth was, "I thought I told you I did not want any crystals, candles, or new age music!"

In a quiet voice I said, "Look Mattie, this is my home, not an office, and people give me crystals as gifts. I think they're quite beautiful. The candles are not lit and the music is one of the essential tools we will be using to get you well. I was not prepared to run around rearranging my home for this session, and eventually you will understand the need for the music."

His only response was, "The name is Matthew." It was a rough start, but a real eye opener for him—and for me. He realized he had to accept the treatment the way it came or go somewhere else, and I was given a glimpse of the anger and intolerance that had brought this man to me.

I asked him what had changed in his life a little over eighteen months ago before being plagued by shingles. He looked at me quizzically. Predictably, he said "Nothing! Absolutely nothing!" as though I were asking him if he had been to Mars lately. I asked him to think again, as I knew there was a cause to all his pain and suffering. He was completely out of balance with no level of peace in his life. The ego mind must have rocked his world hard enough to send him spiraling into anger and sickness.

"Okay," he said, looking at me as though I had just teleported myself into my own living room from another planet and was speaking a language he did not understand. At this point he was not able to comprehend the significance or the destructive conditioning power of his thoughts and his unconscious ego mind programs that were ruining his life.

After looking around the room with its elegant white walls, black granite floors, simple Italian furniture, and its gorgeous blue sea view, and declaring my home looked like a high class bordello, he promptly sat down and said I could start. It was my turn to pause and say, "Okay."

I told him we would be using the same music for every session because he would be creating new neural networks that would help trigger a relaxation response from his brain every time he heard the same music. We went through a complete relaxation technique, and to his surprise, he took to meditation like a duck to water. The first session was a success as far as Matthew was concerned and so he came back a week later.

In the second session he had thought of an answer to my question from the week before. Matthew confessed the only thing that had changed was that a new man had been put on at work around that time.

When I asked him how he felt about that, the flood gates opened. It was like I had just opened one of his software programs that he did not even know existed but was holding him hostage nevertheless. With a mixture of extreme anxiety and aggression, Matthew said he thought the man had been put on to replace him.

We had just met part of the guilty program responsible for taking him out of peace and into declaring war on this new employee—and on himself. Shingles is an autoimmune disease in which the body attacks itself. Matthew was running an ego mind code and was on the attack. He continued to tell me his story. He was 54 years old and afraid of not being able to get another job if he was let go. To make matters worse, Matthew's immediate boss had asked him to help train the new man.

The ego mind jumped right in and created a fantastic story with devastating results. The program ran something like this: I am too old to get another job! Why should I train him to take my job? Who does he think he is, coming in here thinking he can ruin my life? Then every night, as though he had left his computer screen on in his head, the ego mind ran an endless loop of these questions and statements. Matthew could not sleep, and with anxiety levels at an all-time high, he lost equilibrium in every aspect of his life.

He then proudly continued to tell me no one at work liked this man either. Matthew had effectively enrolled everyone else into believing his story and had created a rift between the newcomer and all the other employees as well. "We all

SANDRA AND DANIEL BISKIND

call him Chicken Neck behind his back," he declared with pride. When I asked him how his nemesis had earned the name Chicken Neck, my client replied, "Because he had some kind of cancer and had to have almost half his neck cut away." Wow, the plot thickens and the games become even more painful—for everyone.

Having told his story, Matthew was now calm enough to be able to hear some truths. I asked him had he ever talked to Chicken Neck about what his dreams were for his career. Once again, Mattie looked at me as though I had just come down from the last cloud, and he wanted to know, "What has that got to do with anything?"

I pointed out that Chicken Neck was still there and that he still had his job. It seemed he was not going to be replaced, otherwise it probably would have happened by now. There was reluctant agreement on that point. I asked him if he would consider taking Chicken Neck out to lunch to talk to him about his life and his dreams. "If Chicken Neck has had cancer and lives with this disfiguration, he also has some pretty big ego mind programs to deal with."

This way of thinking was a revelation to him. There is no way Matthew could have connected all the fears and apprehension he was feeling about his work situation with how much he had suffered physically, emotionally, and mentally for nearly two years.

Our hero was learning his lessons the hard way. They come thick and fast when we live in the dualistic world of our illusory tales that the ego mind has conditioned us to believe, and we then perpetuate as the truth. This was a classic example of what happens when we run our stories that we believe are true but are, in fact, pure fantasy.

# LESSONS LEARNED THE HARD WAY

- Matthew's fear and the subsequent anxiety around losing his job and not being able to find another executive position with the same pay grade was followed by...
- Anger at finding himself in this position and constant frustration at not even knowing he was being held hostage by a ruthless set of programs, beliefs, and ideas that had nothing to do with reality.
- The truth completely eluded him as his ego mind kept feeding him a make-believe story that he did not question.
- If you do not question your stories, you will never know the truth. They are only stories and have no meaning in the real world.
- The cause of the problem is seldom what you think it is.
- Believing your perceptions without questions results in projections not based in reality, which creates the platform for mistaken judgments, anxiety, depression, sickness, and even death.
- Neither peace nor truth will ever be found in the stories of the ego mind.

> *"The ego mind is always seeking power because it knows it is powerless to control that which is bigger than itself...your True Self."*
>
> *–Sandra Biskind*

# THE TRUTH REVEALED

Matthew promised he would take Chicken Neck out to lunch that week. At the next session, he was a different man. "Well, I took Chicken Neck to lunch like you suggested and guess what? He does not want my job and never has! He just wanted to be left alone to do his job. You were right. He has really suffered, and we weren't helping things by making his work life a little difficult."

Silently, my ego mind went straight into judgement. "A *little* difficult?"

"I've changed that now," said Matthew, "and we're all getting along just fine. Roger and his wife are coming for dinner next week." Oh! At last, Chicken Neck finally had a name.

Exactly six weeks after Matthew had bravely ventured outside his comfort zone and into my high class spiritual bordello, he rang to tell me the news. Not only was he promoted at work for demonstrating exemplary relationship skills, but he was no longer angry and in pain and could actually sleep with his wife again. She was back in love with our hero, whom she was on the verge of leaving if his ogre-like behavior was not curbed.

Sleep was no longer a problem, and Matthew now meditated every day at home to the music he initially did not want to know about. During our sessions, I would also put my hands on his head to attune him to the Divine white light energy I had been working with for as long as I could remember. This "hands on" regeneration work had him melting with bliss in his chair while it worked its way through his entire system. He was now more of a marshmallow than a hard nut to crack.

In order for Matthew to get the full benefit of our sessions, I recommended he continue to visualize my hands on his head and this white light coursing through his body as often as he could. This continued to attune him to the light of his own True Self, which sped up the regeneration and rejuvenation of his skin and all the cells in his body.

Once his corrupt ego mind programs were revealed and his mistaken perceptions corrected, our hero was now neutral and free to change his relationship with Roger and to regain peace of mind. Doing what he loved to do again without sabotaging himself with his illusory programs, beliefs and ideas, Matthew was no longer a captive of his ego mind and its deadly stories.

Oh, and he no longer suffered from shingles.

"But," Matthew said with a smirk on his face, remembering the first time we met, "that had nothing to do with our sessions."

I laughed, "At least you are still true to form."

# THE "SO WHAT?" CULTURE LIVES ON

Matthew rang soon after in a state of panic. His wife had made plans to bring their eight-year-old grandchild on their annual vacation without talking to him about it first. "I'm not going to cope with this. After all I've been through these past two years, I need a real break."

"Hang on a minute, have you forgotten: *So what? It's okay. It's not real.* I had taught Matthew to say these words like a mantra every time his ego mind began running another story. It is self-talk that instantly takes the edge off anxiety when you lose the feeling of peace around anything. Because the ego mind reacts with total predictability, you can never trust its perceptions and judgements. They will always be based in the illusory world that you have tried to make real lifetime after lifetime.

Matthew was happy to be reminded how easy life can be when he remembered, *It's okay, it's not real, it's only a story, a program to be corrected so I can realign with peace.* Our hero sent me a postcard from his tropical paradise holiday spot.

D. H. 23—"Beach Serene"
Under Tropical Skies, Hollywood, Fla.

*Sandra,*
*Having a great time!*
*The kid is running amuck and all I can*
*say is, the "So What?" culture lives on.*
*Love, Mattie*

Mattie wasn't prepared to stop having private sessions, so we agreed to continue over the phone rather than him spending hours in the car. His life was back on track in a way he never thought possible. His tango with shingles and subsequent change of mind had changed his life forever.

Our hero had discovered the PLATINUM password, which exchanged his ego mind code for the everyday enlightenment code. Mattie loved his new life and was excited about developing this new-found peace—his perfect point of power. His executive position was secure. He was held in high esteem by everyone in the company as his wisdom continued to bring about fruitful initiatives. Matthew had learned these life-changing lessons and knew without a doubt:

- Blindly trusting the ego mind to give him the guidance and wise counsel he sought was no longer a given.
- Believing something to be true did not make it so.
- Just because his perceptions were so capable of projecting his judgments onto any life situation no longer meant he would believe in them.

*"A belief is not only an idea
the mind possesses;
it is an idea that possess the mind."*

—Robert Oxton Bolton

# THE FORGIVENESS FACTOR

Forgiveness, peace, love and joy are inextricably linked. It is only when you have experienced true inner peace that you understand there is another world that exists beyond the ego mind's comprehension. It is an awesome world of wonder and the bliss of pure love.

Pure love is different than the love you feel when the ego mind projects the need to be loved with all its associated programs. In fact, the human mind has always struggled to grasp the enormity of what pure love truly is. Humanity has quite literally buried the light of pure love underneath count-less layers of programs and beliefs within the unconscious mind.

People take drugs for many reasons. One is the desire to recapture the experience of pure love, which the ego mind cannot deliver in its make-believe world. When your mind is overtaken by pure love, you realize there is far more to your existence than what you thought. This is the place peace will take you without the need for anything outside yourself. No drug will reveal the light that lives inside you the way the pure love of the Divine Mind can.

Unlike drugs, many of which will eventually drag you into a living hell or even death, peace will have you gracefully die to the illusions that you have clung to, killed for, and been killed for, over and over again.

**To forgive is the soul's choice that enables you to find peace in a most uncertain world.**

Peace is that place within you where you have given up the attachment to be right. Not about your engineering calculations, your ability to land a plane, or to be a wise counsel, but as one who needs to have his or her personal beliefs accepted no matter what, right or wrong!

Often, when people first start working with us they tell us they want to find peace in their lives. However, they make it clear no matter what we say or do, they will never forgive their mother, or father, or friend who has hurt them. They have their story of pain and suffering and are determined not to let it go. No way, Jose!

They state very clearly that their parent or other family member has hurt them so much that they are not prepared to forgive and forget. It is more important for them to be right and justified in their feeling of pain than move on and be free from the suffering of the past. They were the injured party and they are stuck in their story of abuse. Yet here they were, sitting in a room with two people who were teaching them about enlightenment and love and they thought they could separate forgiveness from the mix.

# YOUR BEST FRIEND, JO

When we are working with people in a live environment, I often begin by telling a wonderful story I heard many years ago, a story about their imaginary friend called Jo. I asked them, as I am asking you now, to use your imagination and pretend you have just left your body. It could be one of those "coming back from the dead" stories if that makes you feel more comfortable.

You find yourself in heaven. Phew! You are given the opportunity to look down over the cloud you just landed on and review your life. This is a prerequisite before you are eligible to return to Earth. You become captivated by the life you have just left. "Look at that!" you say with enthusiasm.

But wait. "Oh no! Look at that." You realize you just have to go back. You were given many opportunities to forgive and, for many so-called valid reasons, you did not take them. You can see your own light growing dimmer every time you were challenged and did not rise to the occasion. If you are ever to have real peace, you realize you need the experience of being able to do it better, of being able to forgive.

You are really excited now because you realize you can undo the damage you caused to your own growth and the growth of others. You want to feel better about who you are becoming, and for that to happen, you need to take the high road and practice forgiveness. And from the looks of the lifetime you are reviewing, you are lucky to have ended up on a cloud at all.

You jump onto the next cloud that floats by and excitedly address a group of people. "Hey, I am so lucky. I get to go back and do things differently. Would anyone be prepared to go back with me and help me?"

"You've got to be kidding. Why would we want to ruin our next lifetime to help you?"

All day long and into the night, you go from one group of people to the next, always getting the same answers. Totally dejected, you finally lift your head.

There, on the furthest cloud, you see your best friend, Jo. Excitement builds once again as you race over to Jo. With an expectant look on your face, you say, "Jo, I just have to go back and fix things. You know I cannot do it on my own. Will you come back with me? Will you help me? Please?"

Jo looks into your eyes with deep love and says to you, "Yes, because I love you so much, I will go back with you, but I have one condition."

"Anything Jo, anything you want."

Jo says, "I will go back with you, but only if when I hurt you— because for you to grow and learn the necessary lessons that come from being able to forgive, I will need to hurt you— you remember who set this up in the first place."

Most people don't speak at this stage. We can literally see the war taking shape in their heads between their ego minds and the wisdom of their hearts.

The head does not want to admit that they could have shattered the peace of the people they have loved and that they are in need of forgiveness. They don't want to admit that they had anything to do with the movie that had played out so convincingly.

**Without unconditional love, forgiveness is still judgement.**

And, forgiveness is easier when you accept we are all the same.

Forgiveness brings you into the peace of the real world of the heart and unconditional love. Ultimately, it brings you to a place where forgiveness is unnecessary because you understand in reality there is nothing to forgive.

In reality there has only ever been unconditional love, and that is who you are.

The heart wins every time when you realize we are actually all one big family and that you have experienced everything in your soul's epic journey on your way out of ego mind's world. The heart understands you have to forgive in order to be forgiven. And again, without unconditional love, forgiveness is still just judgement.

# SLEEPWALKING

Forgiveness enables you to feel compassion for yourself and others. It mercifully stops the flow of mindless accusations and recriminations that can lead to World War III with anyone anytime you feel hurt. Remember, when living in the ego mind world, we are all asleep. What you do when you are sleepwalking is not real. Despite the ego mind's best efforts to make it real, it is still only a dream.

The ego mind is determined for you to hang on to your anger, resentment and stories. These things keep you small and preoccupied in the past, rather than being present, and just perpetuate misery, sickness, and suffering. If you truly desire happiness and success in your relationships, your work and financial life, and the ongoing health and vitality of your body, you must break your ego mind's hold over your life.

To reclaim the enlightened state of your original nature—your True Self—you must replace your ego mind code with its inherent desire to hang on to resentment.

Human nature has become an unconscious mind field that can blow up at any time.

Like Matthew, our executive hero who was not aware of the relationship between his mistaken perceptions, judgments, resentment, and anger to the excruciating pain of shingles, we walk through these mind fields holding on to our stories and subsequent pain at our own peril.

Would you rather be right or be happy?

*"Inner Peace can be reached only when we practice forgiveness. Forgiveness is letting go of the past, and is therefore the means for correcting our misperceptions."*

*–Gerald Jampolsky*

# THE PLAYGROUND

At one of our intensives, a young woman, whose mother had abandoned her as a child and then died before they could find peace with each other, was adamant she could never forgive her mother.

Is there anyone in your life who has died that you have not come to peace with? Do your ego mind programs use these memories to torture you with maddening mind chatter and recriminations of guilt, shame, and of course, blame? Do you feel that you can never forgive them, or yourself, for what was or was not said or done? Odds are there is. The average person responding to this question can name at least three people that still cause inner conflict and feelings of despair and unhappiness.

It's not surprising that one of these people is often a late spouse, one or more parents, other family members, or friends. How do you deal with the lingering, heavy anchor of sorrow and regret that you can't quite shake? The ego mind tells most people it's a hopeless situation and they will never, ever find comfortable closure and inner peace with that person.

Your heart knows what your ego mind will never tell you. You can make peace with this situation and all other stressful issues, including making peace with yourself and those who are still alive yet are clearly candidates to be added to your list, should they expire before you do.

Why not try this creative visualization for yourself? After you read this, close your eyes, breathe deeply, drop your shoulders, take your tongue off the roof of your mouth and become the observer. Now use your imagination and take yourself into a children's playground. This is not the colorful, plastic play areas of today. You are in a park that is full of weeds. The grass is sparse, and it only has a small sand pit, an old wooden seesaw, a slide, and a swing. There are two small children sitting side by side on the old swing set. They don't notice the heavy, rusting link chains; they are just grateful for the blue sky and to be able to play in the sun with their hair flying freely around their faces as they try to soar higher and higher.

At this moment, in this place, these little children finally feel free. They do not have to think about their alcoholic mum or drug-addicted father or the drama or abuse from any family members that awaits them at home.

In this one magical moment in your imaginary playground, whatever mistreatment those small children are suffering is totally forgotten. But wait! Do these little ones look familiar? Ah ha! Of course. It is your mother and your father from their childhood. You realize that when these children—your parents—go home, they are conditioned and programmed to become the people you knew or know today—just like you have been.

During this visualization, walk over to the swing set and sit on the swing. Allow that little girl or little boy to jump up onto your lap. Hold them the way you would hold any precious small child. Look into the eyes of that child—your mother or your father—as they ask the question they so desperately want to ask you. "Please, can you forgive me for ever hurting you in any way? I was only doing what I learned to do and what my parents had learned to do before me."

Now it is up to you. Take a deep breath and focus your attention into your heart. Ask your soul to choose the Divine Mind Code, love them unconditionally, and truly forgive them.

Back in the intensive, as I asked this same question of the woman whose mother who had abandoned her, I could see her face change as she imagined her mother as a little girl on that swing. She held her safely in her arms and heard the child ask for forgiveness. Then she began to cry.

Later, when she shared her experience with the group, she said her mother had appeared before her and told her how sorry she was. As she was sitting in a room supercharged with the energy field of unconditional love, her heart was open to forgiveness. She forgave the one person she thought she could never forgive. They were both able to move on with peace in their hearts. Before the session, although she was attractive, there was a brittleness to this young woman. After her forgiveness experience, she looked softer and more radiant, and everyone could see it.

During these seminars, experiences of forgiveness were a blessing for the whole group. One woman in her 30s said she could never forgive her father for sexually abusing her. She participated in a meditation where her father appeared to her as soon as she closed her eyes. Vehemently, she said to him, "I will never forgive you. Go away."

# TEARS OF LOVE ARE FALLING

He just stood before her with his palms held outward, tears of love falling down his face. Without saying a word, he conveyed his deep regret and sorrow. Her heart melted and in her imagination she held him in her arms. They reassured each other that they were forgiven and were able to trust the process of healing that had just happened. Healthy communication was established for the first time in over 20 years.

It was such a moving experience that everyone in the room was touched by the miracle of true forgiveness. Other people shared similar experiences of how forgiveness had healed their shattered hearts and brought peace to an angry, despairing mind.

Now, back to you. After sitting on that old rusted but reliable swing in the playground of your imagination, how do you feel about forgiving the people who have hurt you?

Are you able to transcend the ego mind, get into your heart, and shift into a state of unconditional love as you forgive the tiny child that was your mom or dad or family member who caused you pain? Right now rate your state on the Integrated Wholeness Scale. Are you at love or above? If so, congratulations! Your whole being is oscillating on the high frequency of love which is positively affecting not only your feelings and your body but the whole of humanity. Thank you!

If you are not at love or above yet, do the visualization again and again until you get there. If you are still having trouble after the third round, you might want to consider a private session with us.

# REVENGE FOR THE RIGHTEOUS

Have you ever been given clear instructions and followed them to the letter only to find your boss or partner was furious with you? Did you ever take the initiative and do something that you knew was the right thing for the company but that someone else with less knowledge and more power thought was wrong? Do you know someone who has been fired for doing what they thought was the right thing and what they thought their boss wanted?

Using the computer metaphor, trying to deal with all your viruses that were created from childhood programming, inherited belief systems, and dysfunctional internal chatter is one thing, but in the ego mind's world, you are constantly interacting with all the viruses of everyone else in your life as well.

Hence, miscommunication is by far the leading cause of mis-understanding and this is a major way the ego mind system perpetuates its dominance. Your perceptions, assumptions, and judgements all work at lightening speed with the same devastating results. When your unconscious programs kick in, they can trigger feelings of impatience, injustice, intoler-ance, pain, and revenge. Remember, it is only the ego mind that would ever deliberately hurt another. The Divine Mind is incapable of intentionally causing suffering.

The Ultimate Mind Shift process works with the True Self to train you to become neutral, to take a step back, and to become stronger than the impulse to hit out.

Have you noticed the people you love and spend the most time with are the people who are most proficient at pushing your buttons, triggering painful events and memories at the speed of light? That's how fast the ego mind activates its painful games. These are the most important ones to practice forgiving, right after you forgive yourself for ever giving power to your corrupted programs of the past.

In the ego mind system, it is hard to keep your mouth shut when the ego mind is running rampant, demanding revenge for the righteous. Ever experienced that? I often say the women in my family were born with foot in mouth disease— including me!

Peace calls for you to delve into the unconditional love of the Divine heart and take each opportunity given you by your friends, family, coworkers, and lovers to forgive. Walk in their shoes for just a moment. Realize their programming, conditioning, life circumstances, and viruses might be different from yours in content but no different in the amount of suffering they cause. They are just as asleep as the rest of us. When you are awake, there really is nothing to forgive— unless you go back to sleep and return to the illusory dream world of the ego mind.

*"If you are irritated by every rub,
how will your mirror be polished?"*

*–Rumi*

# NAVIGATING THE PROCESS OF FORGIVENESS

The words and events that trigger pain and suffering are only the outward manifestations of the unconscious programs coming in to play between the people involved.

You are the star and the writer, director, producer, casting manager, stage hand, lighting technician, composer, and camera operator of your illusory life. When you say, "Action," anything is possible. Just like in *The Bold and The Beautiful*, you've mastered Hollywood's art of immersing yourself in feelings of jealousy, anger, frustration, grief, and despair. Your ongoing TV series entertains you in so many ways, dramatizing your personal programs, past lives, and karma. The ego mind will always script injustice, intolerance, rage and revenge, selfishness, and, of course, the need for constant gratification.

How your ego mind programs create suffering is endless and that is only your TV series. Everyone has been trained by the ego mind to become equally creative in their series.

The people in your life often play the roles you have given them in award-winning style. Unlike the joy of receiving a Nobel Peace Prize for excellence in helping humanity, there are no kudos in the awards given each other for how well you can perpetuate suffering—just battle scars.

# THE FORGIVENESS FACTOR

1. Acknowledge there are ego mind programs at work in the situation. And not only someone else's programs and perceptions, but yours! Take ownership.
2. Reinterpret the situation via the Divine Mind Code instead of the ego mind code. Feel the feelings that you would feel if you knew that the highest and best for all concerned is being realized.
3. Forgive yourself and others for choosing ego mind programs.
4. Peace is restored when forgiveness ends ego mind's dream of conflict.

Forgiveness invites grace, and without its unconditional love forgiveness is still only judgment.

*"Grace is the fullness of God's love."*

*–Sandra Biskind*

# SHOCK TREATMENT

Have you ever written a scene for yourself where you had the experience of saying or doing something that you thought was the right thing, only to have it flung back in your face in a way that leaves you speechless? If so, then you know as the other person reads your script with perfect precision that in such a state of shock it is often impossible to know what to say.

Equilibrium is lost only to be replaced by some degree of suffering. However, a rewrite is in order as the ego mind has plenty to say on the subject once you are alone. Your programs kick into gear and feelings of self-righteousness surface. Left to its own devices, the ego mind will drive you crazy with an all-consuming litany of not only what you should have said, but how rotten the person was who started this roller coaster ride into hell.

A friend was at a party recently where she sincerely congratulated a man on his upcoming award. He had put together a team of people to help fundraise for cancer research. She went into a state of shock when he said, "I didn't think you would congratulate me." Completely nonplussed, she rallied enough to ask why he would say that.

He told her that because he had left his dying brother in her and his sister's care to go on vacation, he assumed she wouldn't think he deserved it. This was only one of the many incidents at that party that pushed her buttons and would have had her in tears had she not gone into a silent rage. She could not leave quickly enough.

In many of the talks I've given people often laugh when I say it is easier to be enlightened and to live a happy, peaceful life when you stay at home alone with your cat. My friend was no exception. She is a wise, deeply spiritual woman who walks through life with an air of peace and calm. When she came to me to talk about the events of that night, she knew she needed help to navigate her way into forgiveness and out of the self-perpetuating shock, anger and confusion of her ego mind.

She was able to laugh when I said it had nothing to do with her.

"It's not about you; it's about the script he has written for himself. You are only an extra and you have obviously forgotten to memorize your lines."

Because the ego mind had the upper hand, it had continued to protest, *But what did I do wrong?* Through the clamor of its shouting she had not considered the fact that he was projecting onto her what he thought about himself. A number of his beliefs were being played out in this one conversation, including:

1. He had not forgiven himself for leaving his cancer-riddled brother to die just so he could have a holiday, and...
2. He would not have forgiven her if the reverse had been true.

A level of peace was restored as the wisdom of her True Self emerged through her understanding heart. The confusion of "What did I do to deserve that?" dissolved when the suffering of her supposed tormentor was exposed. She was then able to rewrite her script so the dramatic storm and choppy waters of unforgiveness gave way to the peace and calm that only true forgiveness brings.

It's not always only about you. You are not the central character in other people's ego mind games. They are!

As you diligently train your ego mind to defer to the wisdom of the Divine Mind, you move into that rarefied air shared by many great leaders. With increasingly higher states of awareness, understanding the big picture and deciphering the codes of others becomes automatic. You know when it is not about you, as well as how to help others who cannot see what you see. This happens for all effective teachers who become a safe haven for others in need.

# SAFE HAVEN IN AN UNCERTAIN WORLD

As you become that safe haven for others in this most uncertain world, the intrinsic feelings of love and joy that come with this high state of peace is the ultimate goal you have been seeking all along. To love who you are and truly forgive is a gift of grace. Within that grace you access the wisdom, strength, and compassion of your True Self. This is where unconditional love and peace reside. This is where you connect to your personal power. It is from here, with love, that you can creatively manifest and experience the life of your dreams.

*You are what you have been looking for.*

Your perfect point of power courses through you as your True Self. It has always existed and always will. It is who you are. It is your beingness that has no needs because everything you could ever need exists within it. What stops you from tapping into the power and the strength of your True Self?

Only the small, mistaken belief that you have separated yourself from your source, from the God of your understanding. This leads us into a world very much like the one Alice fell into. Down the rabbit hole we go, becoming smaller and smaller, our connection to our True Self broken instantly. We find ourselves, like Alice, in a world so alien and so frightening, so distant from the world of the Divine, that we think we will never find our way back home, back into the heart of the Divine.

Having believed the thought of separation and that God has abandoned us, the ego mind perpetuates our unconscious guilt and shame and the mistaken assumption that it is too late to go home. Not only does your Source await your return with open arms, like the prodigal son in the New Testament, but in reality you, your True Self, have never left home except in a dream.

*"Our miscast anger at God has denied us access to our divine power. We can see how our humanness has played such a devastating trick on us."*

–Dr. Valerie Hunt

Daniel and I designed The Ultimate Mind Shift to help you have a deeper, more fulfilling connection to the divinity of your understanding. No matter what your race, creed, religion, or spiritual path, it is time to get back to your divine essence and reclaim your personal power.

Have you ever noticed how charismatic someone is who is happy? They walk into a room and their energy fills the space; they have an authentic smile and they're just irresistible. You know why? Because peace, love, joy and happiness have a very high frequency. And that frequency is so magnetic that no one can resist it.

How much happiness are you experiencing? How much joy? These states need to be experienced in order to share them with others. They come from a place of fullness and are expressions of personal power. If you are not regularly and consistently experiencing peace, love, joy, and happiness, what might be getting in the way?

Like our hero Matthew in the Chicken Neck story, is there something you need to release? Is there a belief or a pattern that is blocking you? Anything that gets in the way of happiness diminishes your ability to experience and express personal power. At the end of the day, it boils down to this: Empowerment = happiness = peace, love, and joy.

*And remember: The key to enlightenment is to lighten up!*

# Laughter

What is laughter? What is laughter?
It is God waking up! O it is God waking up!
It is the sun poking its sweet head out
From behind a cloud
You have been carrying too long,
Veiling your eyes and heart.

It is Light breaking ground for a great Structure
That is your real body—called Truth.

It is happiness applauding itself and then taking flight
To embrace everyone and everything in this world.

Laughter is the Polestar
Held in the sky by our Beloved,
Who eternally says,

"Yes, dear ones, come this way,
Come this way toward Me and Love!

Come with your tender mouths moving
And your beautiful tongues conducting songs
And with your movements—your magic movements
Of hands and feet and glands and cells—Dancing!

Know that to God's eye,
All movement is a Wondrous Language,
And Music—such exquisite, wild Music"

O what is laughter, Hafiz?
What is this precious love and laughter
Budding in our hearts?

It is the glorious sound
Of a soul waking up!

–Hafiz (translated by Daniel Ladinsky)

# UNFULFILLED SEX
# AND DEATH-DEFYING DRUGS

*"Peace is not dependent on finding that elusive something outside yourself."*

*—Sandra Biskind*

The ego mind code activates programs that block your connection to your True Self, which is your spiritual core with its infinite supply of power. When this happens, true confidence goes out the door and low self-esteem and feelings of unworthiness enter so that the body, mind, and soul all suffer. These codes easily have you playing dangerous games with other people that often result in things like unfulfilled sex, date rape, and the mindless use of drugs. Guilt, shame, and blame join the mix and that really limits your ability to shine in the world.

We all experience times when we unconsciously give our ego mind programs power over us. Those are the times when you have lost your connection to the light of your True Self— where real peace resides. You know what that feels like. You no longer feel happy or grateful to be alive, but rather you experience feelings like compulsiveness, entitlement, and self-righteousness.

Have you ever felt a sense of desperation and sought out people, places, or events that might alleviate your pain and recapture some of the joy of where you came from? Searching for love in all the wrong places, have you felt the need to cling to others? Or to entertain yourself with even more scary ideas that distract you from the fact you feel lost in the world? The ego mind would have you depend on it to feel safe and in control, even when you know the opposite is true. In its world, forgiveness has no appeal. Instead, revenge and separation are honored and esteemed as though they were noble elements of your human nature.

The more disconnected from your True Self you are, the harder it is to access your personal power. Like a broken record, lifetime after lifetime, deep down you know that there is something missing.

At some stage we all ask the basic questions about our existence. Why am I here? Where did I come from? What is the point? Where do I belong in this world? Is there a God? Why has God abandoned me? Why is there so much misery, pain, and sickness in the world?

The ego mind's existence is threatened by the truth, and it asks unanswerable questions to keep you distracted by its delusions. When these questions become real for you and are asked on a philosophical level rather than iterated as throw-away lines from a victim mentality, the search for the truth proceeds in earnest. If you are prepared for the truth, the answers are simple. Your journey into your own inner world of light and personal power attracts you like a moth to a flame. You know it is time to climb out of the rabbit hole and leave behind the incredibly eerie world of your own sad and lonely creation and find your way back to where you belong.

In the illusory world of the ego mind, peace, love, forgiveness, and joy have only ever been fleetingly experienced at best. But once tasted, your natural curiosity takes you on the magical, mystical tour into the world of the heart where you will never be satisfied with less. When you get to the truth and neutralize the core beliefs stopping you from accessing your personal power, you can finally become immune to your ego mind programs. Your soul is then free to choose peace, love, joy, and happiness as its baseline as it moves into higher states of awareness.

*"God is the bliss and joy, the peace that dances around and through you when you are no longer ruled by the ego mind... when you are connected to Divine love."*

–Sandra Biskind

# YOU CAN'T TEACH AN OLD DOG
# NEW TRICKS

While creating our resort that was to open in New Zealand's glorious Bay of Islands, we were fortunate to have an excellent cleaner who helped us as we immersed ourselves in yet another new project. As Daniel says, "We have congenital, chronic projectitis and anyone around us had better hope it's not infectious."

One day she complained about her husband's behavior. I jokingly said, "You obviously haven't trained him well enough yet." She shot back, "You can't teach an old dog new tricks." Just as she was in the middle of her pronouncement, Daniel walked into the room. As I looked at him I could feel my whole face light up. Turning to her, with great conviction I said, "Of course you can! Look, here's my young puppy in an old dog's body." Luckily Daniel's sense of humor was still intact and he thought it was cute to be called a young puppy in an old dog's body. We all laughed.

One of the many amazing traits that Daniel possesses is his curiosity and unquenchable thirst for learning. He can assimilate and incorporate information into his life in a nanosecond, and does not come across as an arrogant know-it-all. He has made my happiness his highest priority and is eager to adapt wherever possible—a very sexy trait in a man, as any woman will tell you, and an incredible role model for me. From Daniel, I learned the biggest secret to having a great relationship: **Make your partner's happiness your highest priority.**

# ONE OF THE SEXIEST TRAITS
# ON THE PLANET

Do you ever feel like your life is a series of failing relationships? Have you ever felt like you are invisible at work or at a party where you really wanted to impress your boss or partner? Maybe you are running a program that is blocking you from accessing your personal power, charisma, curiosity and confidence.

Perhaps as a child you heard someone older say to you, "*You don't know what you are talking about. Give others a chance to answer the questions. Stop talking.*" The ego mind creates new programs as it stores this information as fact in the unconscious.

If it was an event surrounded by emotion, the program can become controlling. If your reaction involves making a decision around that topic in an emotionally charged state, that can become a controlling program with an almost uncrackable code.

Can you identify with any of these programs? Too much knowledge is dangerous. Don't make a sound. Don't stand out. Keep small. Keep quiet. Don't rock the boat. No one is interested in what you've got to say! Codes like these block your ability to self-assess, to be teachable and to shine.

We have always admired people with the willingness and ability to keep learning, to be teachable, and who have unquenchable curiosity. Teachable people are self-reflective and adaptable. They know the importance of self-awareness and mindfulness. They work on themselves because they're on their own inner journey and understand the importance of looking at what is going on for them and seeing where they need to change.

*Teachable people display authentic accountability.*

They answer questions like, "What's my role?" and "Why has this triggered anger and resentment?" with "I've got to work on myself" and "How can I work on this to make this relationship better?" They are not afraid to have honest conversations with themselves and their partners, bosses, or family members. They hold themselves accountable and take 100% responsibility. They want to be the best version of themselves.

No matter what age, race, gender, financial situation, or political orientation, it is still one of the most exciting traits any person can have. When you meet someone who has become a master in their field, or they are just starting a new project, they are often open and passionate about the huge learning curve they are on. You can feel it in the power and excitement of their speech and body language. The frequency they are on is infectious. It is a real turn-on and in many cases others end up wanting to go along for the ride.

Like learning to understand your own inner language and codes, a new project can be a major undertaking, especially when you have not been in that industry before. Both Daniel and I are now in our third careers. Every step of the way since we started in business—Daniel in his early 20s and I at age 18—we have been blessed to have people mentor us and invest time and energy in us and our endeavors.

You could tell they were excited by our precociousness, and often our innocence and naivete, as well as by the creative ideas that made our businesses so successful. Just as we were excited and honored to be working with these incredibly talented and successful people, they wanted to be a part of our lives. They were uplifted and inspired by that wonderful, saturated spirit we were exhibiting in our work and projects—our insatiable curiosity and teachability.

*"I have no special talent.*
*I am only passionately curious."*

*–Albert Einstein*

We consistently take to heart and follow through on the direction and coaching that are so generously offered to us. The more we learn, the more excited and passionate we become. And, the more confidence, curiosity, and "can-do" attitude we exhibit, the more people gravitate to us. Accountability, passion, confidence, the ability to change your mind on a dime, and the ability to love and forgive as you continue to learn and grow are traits that are super attractive to people.

They are a common denominator of people who live a PLATINUM life and are continually becoming the best version of themselves. If you take looks out of the equation, all those qualities are by far some of the sexiest traits on the planet.

Lawrence A. Appley was a member of the board of Daniel's company and one of his most admired mentors. He was a recipient of the Presidential Medal of Merit and his legendary presidency and chairmanship of the American Management Association spanned four decades. His professional success and his wonderfully loving relationship with his wife both correlated with his insatiable appetite and ability to learn. Being teachable was second nature for Larry. He would often say he could not go to bed at night until he had learned something new that day. He was always looking at how he could better himself—in other words, to become the best version of himself.

He was obviously curious, teachable, confident, and knowledgable. Larry Appley generously shared his wisdom, knowledge, and genuine interest in others and his demonstrated action created a magnetic force that made him irresistibly attractive. Into his 80s, he had that twinkle in his eyes and the sparkle of someone who understood that every day held the promise of inner growth and of learning something new.

We had a memorable conversation with Jack Canfield, the author of the best selling *Chicken Soup for the Soul* series and *The Success Principles* and a featured teacher in the film *The Secret*. With real interest he asked us how our work was different from anything else he had experienced. I was explaining how by tapping into the human mind field we accessed information that enabled us to resolve our clients' core issues that were blocking them from being able to succeed in any area of their lives. We described how the CODE-BREAKER PLATINUM password was used to shift awareness and bring about enlightened states of consciousness. I was obviously passionate about the topic and typically speaking quite fast.

He missed something I said, and instead of letting it slide, he was so engrossed and interested in the conversation that he wanted me to go back and repeat it. I immediately said, "I'm sorry, I was speaking too fast." He looked at me with a smile on his face and said, "No, I just need to listen faster."

Daniel and I looked into each others eyes and knew we were thinking and feeling the same thing. Jack's confidence and charisma is unmistakable but when he said that, his attraction went to a whole new level. We were in love!

Where would you rather meet your friends or prospective partner? In a bar where you are more likely to find ego-driven agendas, or where you have a better chance of making a connection that transcends those agendas—perhaps a library, a book club, or at a workshop or live event being hosted by high consciousness people teaching you about new levels of awareness, or any other of your favorite topics?

One young man we know married a woman he met in a bar. She was drunk and crawling under his table. The marriage only lasted a year before it started to unravel. He told us he couldn't understand why she drank every night and became another person, but her demonstrated action right from the first night they met was really all the answer he needed. He married that other person, but expected something very different.

I know for a fact that some of my older male friends were wisely advized to go to libraries to meet women in their age group. What fun! To all those older women who thought you were going to the library to study or do research or find the next book for your book club, you might get more than you bargained for—and love it.

Has anyone ever told you that you were smart, interesting, or exciting? If so, they are probably thinking, "Wow, you are so sexy."

If you have not developed these traits in your life maybe it is time to get on the "sexiest traits on the planet" track. Discover and neutralize the programs that are stopping you from shining, from becoming the best version of you so you can transform your personal and business relationships and live a PLATINUM life. Yes, no matter how young or how old you are, being curious and teachable is a turn on. Being accountable and responsible, not blaming others for how you feel, and looking inside to find and neutralize the guilty programs is incredibly attractive.

# TRAINING TOOLS:
# MEDITATION AND VISUALIZATION

On your quest to attain peace, you can use meditation and various forms of visualization to retrain your mind and help your brain rewire itself. This helps create new habits that not only lead to better health and vitality but are prerequisites to integrating your unconscious, conscious, and supercon-scious states of awareness. In your PLATINUM life. this is known as Wholistic Consciousness, which we explore in the third book in this series, *AWARENESS: Discover How Life Really Works.*

Meditation, visualization, and other techniques that attune you to higher frequencies have been used for thousands of years as rungs on the ladder out of the darkness of the rabbit hole into the light of the Divine Mind.

Many years ago, I was asked by a group of nuns to come to their retirement home and teach them meditation. I had no idea nuns retired, but of course they only retired from profes-sionally helping people, not from their calling to know their God. It was such a special experience for me and hopefully for them, too.

There they were, all in their mid-60s and older, still wearing their black and white habits. I couldn't help myself. I felt like Whoopi Goldberg in the movie *Sister Act.* Luckily for every-one and especially me, I wasn't there to teach them to sing! In unison, they closed their eyes and began to breathe deeply and relax as they followed my voice. What an incredible sight. Have you ever looked at your beloved or child when they were sleeping? Remember how your heart expanded and their loveliness almost took your breath away? That is exactly how I felt in that moment, looking at these incredible women who all still wanted to learn and grow and deepen their connection to God.

After the first session, I asked them why they wanted to learn to meditate. The answer was, "To get closer to God; to know the peace of God better." The unsaid implication from their tones of voice and facial expressions was, "Well, why else would we want to meditate?" Without ever having formally meditated, they instinctively knew that meditation is a way into the peace of the Divine Mind as it progressively undoes the world of the ego mind.

It is also a proven way to alleviate the stress and tension that builds in your body causing distress, dysfunction, and disease. A growing number of companies around the world make time for their employees and managers alike to take small meditation breaks. Airline pilots on British Airways have long been taking mandatory ten-minute meditation breaks for revitalization before landing.

Like meditation, visualization relaxes the body to change your state, and it then uses the imagination to bring about purposed outcomes. The military uses the power of visualization to create efficiency, effectiveness, and confidence. The habit of having achieved something in the mind translates to success in the field.

Visualization can open doors into the unconscious mind where you can delve into your inner world and create new habits and associations that serve you. As you create new habits, you create new neural pathways in your malleable brain, making it easier to maintain your desired new behaviors.

Both meditation and visualization can take the physical brain waves down into the frequencies known as Delta and Theta. That is where, just like babies and young children, we access, learn, and absorb information more easily, like sponges. Theta, 4 to 8 cycles per second, is just above the lowest frequency of Delta, 0.5 to 4 cycles per second.

Babies are in a constant meditative-like state as their brains predominately operate in the Delta range until about age two. A child's brain begins to oscillate at the higher Theta frequency between two and six. This is the time you learn and process the enormous amount of information that will set you up to live in the physical world you have just entered. The senses of babies and children constantly send messages into a brain oscillating at what could be called the programming frequency, or in the case of your mind training, you might call it the reprogramming frequency.

What you see, hear, feel, taste, and touch from your parents and extended families is absorbed directly by the unconscious mind where these observations become programs, beliefs, and ideas that literally have the power to change your biological structure. As studies in psychoneuroimmunology have discovered, they can make you sick or keep you well and can be even more potent variables than your genetic inheritance.

Have you ever experienced an unaware teacher, parent, or sibling say things like: "Stupid child! You've got no hope," or "Children should be seen and not heard," or "Who do you think you are? You're too big for your britches." These plant seeds that your unconscious mind processes as truth. The untrained minds of babies and children have neither the wisdom nor the capacity to sort truth from fiction. Even unintentionally, these abusive seeds produce the weeds of corrupted programs that can drastically impact your destiny.

The good news is that meditation and visualization can help you discover and rehabilitate the damaged plants that grew from the corrupted seeds of your childhood. You can neutralize debilitating beliefs and end the suffering they cause once and for all. We talk more about this gift and the process of becoming neutral in the sixth book in this series, *NEUTRALITY: Go Beyond Positive—Your Key to Freedom* and introduce its basic steps later on in this book.

We invite you to visit www.TheBiskinds.com for your free meditation downloads. You can also go to The CODEBREAKER WORKBOOK: BOOK TWO in THE CODEBREAKER SERIES to delve deeper into the techniques and benefits of using meditation and visualization with PLATINUM as your guide. It will be available mid-2015.

The good news is it is in your hands. No matter how many personal development books you read and success manuals you study, unless you attain peace, which is reached by neutralizing your ego mind stories that have you stuck in a holding pattern of old beliefs, you will not realize the personal changes you seek or the life you aspire to live.

# TRAINING GOALS

It is time for your soul to awaken and retrain itself to choose the Divine Mind Code to guide you into the state of peace with love and forgiveness. You naturally make this choice when you break the ego mind code, which automatically enables access to your True Self and the Divine Mind Code.

**SURRENDER TO NOT KNOWING**: Surrender to the fact the ego mind does not know the truth. Even when you are certain you know something, remember it is only an opinion colored by the perspective of your programs. A belief is just an opinion you've habitually elevated in your ego mind.

**IT'S JUST ANOTHER STORY**: Discover what is stopping you from changing the way you think. It is either an unconscious or conscious ego mind program that stops you from being able to get neutral and change your thinking.

**MASTER YOUR MOUTH**: Give yourself a break and put the forgiveness code into play in your life. It is so easy to mindlessly think and then speak hurtfully. When you master your mouth, you only have to forgive yourself rather than ask forgiveness of others.

**MASTER YOUR THOUGHTS**: Master your thoughts and you master your whole world.

**ENLIGHTENED SELF-INTEREST**: Make forgiveness your highest priority. Move on to the next adventure without allowing the pain of the past to be the pain of your future. Neutralize the ego mind programs stopping you from accessing your personal power. This is enlightened self-interest at its best.

*"True Forgiveness
is the prerequisite
to inner peace."*

*–Sandra Biskind*

# EGO PUPPY TRAINING #1: PEACE

Now, just for fun, imagine your ego mind is your new puppy. Its name, of course, is Ego Puppy. It has already learned some terrible tricks from the rest of the litter, the untrained mother, and the mostly-absent father. When you first bring it home, you are convinced it has been roaming wild for centuries. It is hard to believe it could have learned such obnoxious behavior in only a few months. It is already ruining the carpet; chewing slippers, sneakers, and your most cherished items; stealing food; and regularly keeping the whole neighborhood up all night with its whining and barking. Like the puppy Marley in the movie *Marley and Me,* it brings chaos and one crisis after another into your life.

It is overwhelming to contemplate how much there is to do in undoing little Ego Puppy's attachment to trouble. Deep down inside, you know no one else can do it for you. (After all, it really is your ego mind we are talking about.) So you simply must make a start. But take one step at a time, because Ego Puppy would eat Marley for breakfast when it comes to mischief and mayhem.

As usual, your ego mind has the audacity to complain to itself. *What did I do to deserve this? Why isn't there someone else to handle the job?* When the complaining finally ceases, you discover the answer. Absolutely everybody got a member of Ego Puppy's litter at the same time! The best way to proceed is to find someone who has already made a start and is proficient in training puppies just like little Ego. To realize your puppy's full potential could take multiple trainers, numerous books, and several different instruction methods. It will require you to be diligent in the process of undoing little Ego's well-known habitual behavior, but never lose sight of your goal. The rewards are what makes life worth living.

As luck would have it, you also got your baby kitten at the same time. You named this baby Karma Kitten and it has four eyes: one physical pair and one spiritual pair—a source of your intuition. You will learn more about your need for the wise and intuitive Karma Kitten later in this series.

As training finally begins to progress, the stress and suffering caused to everyone in your human family begins to ease off. Your body, mind, and soul relax enough to find new vitality and strength in a world that is starting to return to peace. And, you can start to love yourself for who you really are rather than who you became when Ego Puppy first trotted into existence.

Unlike in the movie, where the family grieved Marley's death, when Ego Puppy graduates with honors as a summa cum laude service dog, there will be cosmic fireworks as you celebrate the love and companionship of your best friend, and then your return to peace.

There are ways of helping yourself experience peace in this world of endless drama. To break the hold of the ego mind, you must train the mind by practicing new ways of thinking. When you train the ego mind to sit and stay you move into new levels of awareness. Through repetition you create a habit field and cause the brain to create new neural pathways, which become increasingly dominant. The old pathways reflect your programming from lifetimes of conditioning. They habitually force you back into the same thought processes responsible for the belief that your ego mind programs are the truth.

*"You become what you think about."*

*–Earl Nightingale*

Okay, so now you know your ego mind is like a new puppy. We do not want to crush it or destroy it. It came into your life as a baby when you were born and has all the needs of any baby. As science has discovered, we all need constant love and attention to reach our full potential as loyal, loving, well-adjusted members of any family. Out of love and enlightened self-interest, you begin to ensure ongoing peace in your life when you take responsibility for training the newest member of the family—your newly recognized ego mind.

Your rewards are huge. They go beyond the healing effects this loving relationship has on you emotionally and mentally. Even your overall health and well being on a physical level are also impacted positively. You now have a best friend—someone who could even save your life.

When ego puppies feel the love you have for them they know they are safe in the world and become receptive to training. By repetition and reward, your much-loved ego puppy quickly learns to ask to go outside to relieve itself. It also learns appropriate behavior from the games you play together. The puppy wants the applause to continue and it learns from the training sessions how it needs to act in the world to keep the love coming.

If an older, well-trained dog is in the equation, the puppy will learn how its done from them, or how it's not done from a naughty older compatriot. Then you have double the trouble.

# JUMPSTART THE PROCESS

The CODEBREAKER PLATINUM Series presents a systematic process that you can adapt to suit your own needs and lifestyle to power up your life. It contains a wide range of simple tools, techniques, and practices that all complement and reinforce one another. They fall into the two categories that encompass all fundamental approaches to inner development in every spiritual and personal development tradition: inquiry and attunement.

**INQUIRY** practices are those in which you ask yourself questions.

**ATTUNEMENT** practices are those in which you harmonize your own frequency with a frequency of your choice.

**INQUIRY**: To start, we present three simple but powerful inquiry techniques: The Four Questions, Rate Your State and the Quantum Neutrality Process. Empowered neutrality is where you consistently correct emotional blocks that stop you from living the best version of you. To get you started, we have outlined the first easy steps so you can correct emotional blocks and go from feeling awful to awesome in minutes.

**ATTUNEMENT**: Reading this series of books attunes you to the enlightenment frequency as does working with us at our live events and our recorded and online programs. Another attunement practice we strongly recommend is meditation. We offer you a link to a guided meditation on PEACE on our website www.TheBiskinds.com which you are welcome to download and use as often as you can.

We suggest using it at least once daily.

The more you use these tools, the more you will get from them. Not only will you become more skillful in their use but their impact is cumulative.

This is an introduction to a lifelong system that can take you as far and deep and as high on the Integrated Wholeness Scale as you are prepared to go. Have fun! And remember, your thoughts are the only thing stopping you from having the life you want.

*"Man is a credulous animal and must believe something. In the absence of good grounds for belief, he will be satisfied with bad ones."*

*–Bertrand Russell*

# THE FOUR QUESTIONS: PEACE

This inquiry technique utilizes your internal GPS. It is based on the use of mindfulness, which is simply observing yourself without judgment. It is intentional self-awareness. This simple but powerful tool cultivates your emotional intelligence.

Use your feelings as your readout on your internal GPS. The more negative you are feeling the more off course you are. The better you feel the more on course you are. Making repeated course corrections is an easy and effective way to change your state.

Use it to connect with your true north, your True Self.

Use this simple set of questions to change the way you feel from one moment to the next. As you practice and become proficient, this technique will become second nature and you will use it like an aircraft's auto-pilot to course-correct automatically. Use it whenever you feel yourself moving away from your natural state of peace and love. Recognize that is only untrained ego mind mischief at play.

Answer the questions truthfully and spontaneously. Stay focused on the answer to question number four for as long as you can.

This is an example only.

Use your own words and the wisdom of your own heart to answer the questions.

1. **What am I feeling?**
   I feel angry and frustrated.

2. **What am I focused on?**
   They are wrong and they should do what I think is right.

3. **How do I want to feel?**
   Peaceful and balanced.

4. **What focus will serve that?**
   Letting go of the need to be right, noting what we share in common, and accepting responsibility for my feelings.

As you breathe deeply, stay focused in your heart, and with love, immediately forgive anything that pushes your buttons and brings up a program to be corrected and neutralized. Be grateful for the opportunity to become more whole by clearing out yet another unwanted belief or idea that takes you away from peace.

# RATE YOUR STATE: PEACE

Use these three questions as a guide to rate your state and discover which code you are operating in:

## 1.) Is there someone in your life you have not forgiven?

Odds are, when you have not forgiven someone, this takes up a lot of rent-free space in your mind. Ego mind makes you into a martyr and often drives you crazy by rerunning the same scenario over and over again. You are then low on the Integrated Wholeness Scale.

## 2.) Have you forgiven yourself for hurting someone else?

The ego mind is quick to make you wrong and punish you for any slip in your magnificence. Become aware of how your words and thoughts are capable of creating pain for others and ultimately for yourself. Train the ego mind to sit on the sidelines as you bring your True Self back into play where real forgiveness always wins the day. You rate high on the Integrated Wholeness Scale when you forgive your ego mind programs and empower yourself to adjust your thinking.

## 3.) When was the last time you stopped yourself from judging someone else?

Every time you judge someone else, you have given ego mind the free rein it wants. You cannot know what someone else is going through until you walk in their shoes. Judgments and all forms of separation (including gossip!) keep you low on the Integrated Wholeness Scale.

Using your new CODEBREAKER PLATINUM passwords activates your personal power and facilitates tolerance, acceptance, and forgiveness—which is the way to Peace. You are now moving higher on the Integrated Wholeness Scale.

# THE ULTIMATE MIND SHIFT: AN INTRODUCTION TO QUANTUM NEUTRALITY—THE FIRST STEPS

**It's time to power up your life.**

The Quantum Neutrality Process is the art and science of identifying and neutralizing your blocks and deleting their effects, thus restoring strength and energy to body, mind, and soul. This empowers you to make shifts in your awareness, access your personal power, and make better decisions about life, love and your relationships.

**1. Your information center is your midline, core, spine, and your central and peripheral nervous systems. The components of your information center can be corrected to be strong by closing your eyes and imagining more of your True Self in the form of white light pouring in through the top of your head and filling your whole being. If you are not seeing or feeling the light, don't quit! Keep going until you do; simply use your imagination. Remember a time you sat with the sun pouring through you or felt the heat of a spotlight on your head. If you are still not connecting to the white light, take yourself into the sunshine or sit under a hot spotlight. That's it. You can do this!**

*As you imagine your True Self in the form of white light filling your being, this corrects the information center, relaxes you and informs the ego mind it is time to sit and stay; to listen and learn without comment.*

**2. Discover the issue responsible for taking you out of balance by tapping into your intuition. Intuition is a core element of higher awareness. It is the powerhouse within your mainframe. It identifies passwords and deciphers faulty codes running in your human computer. Your intuition is used to access information from the Divine Mind field and helps you determine where you are weak or strong. What is the answer? Concentrate. Focus. Determine to access your intuition and have it work for you.**

*How many times have you experienced this? Say you're doing a Google search and after only one word, or even just a part of a word, the computer appears to read your mind and in a flash complete thoughts appear. Intuition works in a similar way. The Divine Mind assembles millions of life experiences and provides you with an immediate "Executive Summary."*

*Intuition is always ready for your use. Some people call it a gut feeling or inner knowing. The more you use it, the stronger it gets and the more effective your corrections become. Your intuition can identify what programs make you feel weak or strong, but if you do not trust it yet, use muscle testing or kinesiology to confirm the source of the weakness.*

*When you feel discomfort such as fear, negativity or pain a program has been triggered and you need to get neutral. You might think you know what needs to be worked on, but in every case it is never what you think it is. All disease, distress and discomfort first originates within the mind field and only then is felt as pain. As a small child you brought programs into your life with you as well as acquiring them from your environment.*

*The cause is always found in an ego mind program which shows up as a belief or idea. Usually you will not identify or even relate with the original programs as they have been buried deep in the storage section—the unconscious mind—of your computer for so long you have forgotten they were even there.*

**3. Applying the Quantum Neutrality Process, focus on your information center and say, either aloud or to yourself, "I neutralize all beliefs, ideas, and patterns associated with this program on a physical, mental, emotional, psychological, psychic, or spiritual level." Your intention will determine your results. Don't just say it. Feel it. Mean it.**

**4. Now say aloud or to yourself, "I delete all karma and habitual thinking related to this program." Feel it and visualize it leaving your body. Feel the weight lifting off your shoulders.**

**5. With unconditional love, forgive everyone and everything that has hurt you associated with the program you have just corrected, including yourself. Even if you have to start with just one person and a small or trivial issue, forgive everyone and everything involved.**

As you follow these steps, the emotional charge around the information in the program dissolves. In fact, you will not be able to find the old emotional feelings and reactions once they have been corrected. Often you will feel a shift in your body once the relevant mental and emotional energy has been discharged in this way.

A feeling of relief is the first sign the program has been corrected and you are neutral to the event. You will feel empowered to move forward, free of the blocks to your inner peace. Your body, mind, and soul will now realign with your personal power and you will be more able to regenerate, rejuvenate, strengthen, and renew your entire energy system.

This is an introduction to Quantum Neutrality, a groundbreaking process that is invaluable and life-changing. We treat it more fully in *NEUTRALITY: Go Beyond Positive—Your Key to Freedom*, the sixth book in The CODEBREAKER PLATINUM Series. We also address this in still more depth in our programs, trainings, and live events.

# A QUICK OVERVIEW: PEACE

*"We can never obtain peace in the outer world until we make peace with ourselves."*

*–Dalai Lama*

- PEACE is the state of harmony and balance, tranquility and quiet, in which the highest good for all is naturally sought.
- In this state of serenity you are free from unsettling thoughts and emotions. Inner peace is the power source that enables your journey into a PLATINUM life.
- When your soul chooses to live by the ego mind code instead of the Divine Mind Code, you are out of alignment with your True Self, which always results in a lack of inner peace.
- By disconnecting from your natural state of peace, you open the door to mental, emotional, and physical distress of all kinds. For example, feelings of despair, grief, and panic and a disconnection from those you love can over-power your life with devastating results.
- If you do not question your stories, you will never know the truth. They are only stories and have no meaning in the real world.
- The truth is never what the ego mind thinks it is.
- Believing your perceptions without question creates pro-jections not based in reality, which then creates the plat-form for mistaken judgments, anxiety, depression, sick-ness, and even death.
- Neither peace nor truth will ever be found in the stories of the ego mind.

- Peace, love, joy, and forgiveness are inextricably linked.
- Peace is not dependent on finding that elusive something outside yourself.
- Peace is found in that place within you where you have given up your need to be right and the need to fight for your fear-based beliefs.
- It is easy to forgive when you accept that you are the same as everyone else—and they are the same as you.
- Forgiveness enables you to feel compassion for yourself and others.
- As you step into your personal power, you understand that true forgiveness is the only way to peace. The feelings of love and joy for yourself and others that come with true forgiveness are all the reward you will ever need.
- Peace calls for you to delve into the unconditional love of the Divine Mind and take every opportunity given you by friends, family, co-workers, and lovers to forgive.
- Peace is not something you have to create in the real world; it already exists within the heart and mind of your True Self. All you need to experience it is to correct the ego mind programs blocking it.
- Your perfect point of power courses through you. It has always existed and always will. It is accessed through peace.
- Fear, and everything associated with fear, is born from within the isolated womb of your compromised beliefs and is not real.
- The Divine Mind is the ever-expanding, infinite expression of pure love and joy that expresses itself deep within you when you are no longer held hostage by the ego mind but are free and at peace.
- Only when you are at peace and you are fully present— not numb or asleep, but fully awake—do you experience life directly, free of the influence and filters of ego mind programs, ideas, and beliefs.

- To be in a state of peace you need to be in harmony with the energy frequency of peace. To attune to this frequency consistently it is helpful to set the stage for peace in your home and work and essential to train your mind and create new habits.

Some simple steps to accomplish this:

- On your inner journey into peace, use mindful meditation daily. Become the observer of your thoughts and feelings without comment or judgment—odds are you will discover emotional triggers that will need to be corrected so you can be the neutral observer in a place of peace.
- Make your home and work space as harmonious as possible. Use your creativity and intuition to create a stable, peaceful environment to work, play, and love in. For instance, you could have art depicting beautiful places in nature, or just gorgeous washes of color—anything that makes you feel inspired and at peace. If your rooms are small or dark, place mirrors opposite the windows to reflect the light and create the illusion of space. Every home I have ever lived in I have painted white, but you could paint your walls your favorite colors. Make sure you declutter your floors and bench and countertops. Spirit loves beauty in all forms. That is why the more you create beautiful spaces around you the more peaceful, uplifted, and content you will feel.
- As often as possible visit a place in nature where you can enjoy the beauty and serenity of your surroundings. Take in the splendor of a sunset or sunrise and allow yourself to feel the joy of being alive in that moment.
- Get your blood flowing and oxygenate your entire system. Develop the habit of deep diaphragmatic breathing. Exercise as often as you can: walk, run, dance, lift weights, or just tense and relax. Center yourself and connect with your core essence by practicing yoga, tai chi, or any of

the martial arts that train you to find fluidity, balance, and strength through a state of inner peace.

- Continually use inquiry—like in Rate Your State, The Four Questions and The Quantum Neutrality Process—to stay balanced and mindful and to heighten your level of awareness.
- To experience inner peace you need to forgive. Remember, you are only ever forgiving ego mind programs—both your own and others'—that have been accumulated since birth.
- Often people want forgiveness to be a mutual exchange. It's not! It's unilateral. Forgiveness is intensely personal and it depends on unconditional love.
- Use the creative visualisation from the story THE PLAYGROUND. Go back in time and truly forgive anyone, including yourself, who has hurt you.
- True inner peace is not dependent on external circumstances. Paradoxically, it is the state in which you can exert the most constructive influence on external circumstances.

We are inviting you to make the Ultimate Mind Shift—the shift from the head to the heart; from the ego mind code to the Divine Mind Code. As Deepak Chopra said, "The movement of life is from duality to unity." This is a total paradigm shift. It is the true key to inner peace and to living a PLATINUM life of happiness and love, success and joy.

Do not let your ego mind programs steal your peace.

**REMEMBER:**
**IT'S OKAY. IT'S NOT REAL. IT'S JUST YOUR STORY.**

*"Reality is merely an illusion, albeit a very persistent one."*

–Albert Einstein

"Until one is committed there is hesitancy, the chance to draw back, always ineffectiveness. Concerning all acts of initiative (and creation), there is one elementary truth, the ignorance of which kills countless ideas and splendid plans:

That the moment one definitely commits oneself, then Providence moves too. All sorts of things occur to help one that would otherwise never have occurred. A whole stream of events issues from the decision, raising in one's favor all manner of unforeseen incidents and meetings and material assistance, which no man could have dreamt would have come his way.

I have learned a deep respect for one of Goethe's couplets:

Whatever you can do, or dream you can—begin it. Boldness has genius, power, and magic in it."

–W. N. Murray
*The Scottish Himalayan Expedition, 1951*

You are now ready to move on to the next keyword in The CODEBREAKER PLATINUM Series. As you move forward on life's greatest adventure and you build upon PEACE as your foundation, it is time to take the next step in connecting with who you really are—which is Love.

**LOVE**: Unconditional love is your essence.
Your purpose is to create and evolve and
have fun expressing the love that you are.

***LOVE****: Ignite the Secret to Your Success* is the next book in The CODEBREAKER PLATINUM Series. Use it to strengthen your connection with your True Self and the energy frequency of enlightenment.

Access the tools and resources at www.TheBiskinds.com.

http://thebiskinds.com/peace     ***PEACE****: Power Up Your Life*
http://thebiskinds.com/love      ***LOVE****: Ignite the Secret to Your Success*

*With warmest love and blessings,*
*Sandra and Daniel*

# ABOUT SANDRA AND DANIEL

The Biskinds share their expertise in personal transformation as thought leaders, authors, teachers, professional speakers, and consultants. They are also coaches and mentors. Both have had highly successful careers as business entrepreneurs with multi-award winning businesses in the United States of America, Australia, and New Zealand.

Now based in the USA and focused exclusively on personal transformation, Sandra and Daniel are the originators of a groundbreaking body of work introduced in *The CODE-BREAKER PLATINUM Series.* Presented with passion, intensity, grace, and wisdom, the Series is designed to empower individuals to build their own life of happiness, success, and fun—putting passion back into relationships, fulfillment and joy back into work, and restoring and enhancing health, vitality, and well-being.

Born in Australia, Sandra has always been an intuitive who spoke to Divine beings from the age of three when she told her mother she was here to work for God. Even through 36 death-defying surgeries, financial ruin, and divorce Sandra's determination to succeed and to find the answers to the eternal questions of life, death, and love led her to become a self-made millionaire by the age of 29. She has diligently worked with some of the greatest spiritual teachers and success coaches throughout the world and is now a highly sought-after keynote speaker and workshop leader in personal transformation and enlightenment.

Born in America, Daniel's dream has always been to set people free. To do that, he realized he first had to set himself free. Daniel had a 25-year career as owner/CEO in large scale property development with high profile roles in civic, charitable, and industry leadership positions. His training encompassed a wide variety of spiritual traditions and deep experience in the human potential movement as well as advanced business and management education. Sharing his spiritual journey has been the major theme of his life.

When he met an Australian woman at one of her seminars in New Zealand, Daniel knew Sandra would rearrange his life forever. He proposed to her on their first date and they agreed to be married the next time they met. Sixteen years later, they still consider themselves newlyweds.

In their first project together they created a private retreat on a power place in New Zealand to host spiritual intensives which, in its first year following completion, won *Condé Nast Traveller*'s highest rating in its Gold List of the world's Top 100 Hotels. It went on to be crowned the world's best luxury coastal hotel by the World Luxury Hotel Awards in 2010. In 2013, Eagles Nest received the World Travel Awards title of The World's Best Luxury Villa Boutique Resort.

Sandra and Daniel work with highly successful people who are committed to get to the next level in their business and private lives—to be the best versions of themselves. Their clients are determined to successfully lean into their lives—aware, mindful, and present.

**From Sandra and Daniel:** *Your thoughts are always the key variable in every situation. Training your mind to think thoughts that serve you is your highest priority, and becoming the best version of you is the most rewarding undertaking of all. It is an open-ended process in which we are continually* reminded that the means and the ends must always be in harmony and integrity.

We have dedicated our lives to sharing our journey into enlightenment and wholeness. We invite you to share yours with us and move into higher and higher states of Integrated Wholeness together—to truly become the best versions of ourselves.

On our journey, we have invested many decades in study, research, and development. We have traveled the planet to sit with many leading spiritual teachers and energy masters and in the process have developed a turbo-charged process for rapid change which results in major shifts within minutes as we neutralize blocks. We constantly witness people set free from the debilitating residue of trauma that years of therapy and counseling have been unable to shift. Using the higher awareness of Wholistic Consciousness, we tap into what scientists call the human mind field to identify the underlying causes of any issue and then use precise frequencies to neutralize them and delete their effects.

Like most people, we have had massive challenges throughout our lives. Using the work we teach, we have not only survived but thrived. For more than 30 years, we have successfully worked with thousands of people around the world and been gratified to achieve amazing results. We invite you to use us and these books as loving guides, mentors, and coaches to support you on your journey.

You now have unprecedented opportunity and resources to make a quantum leap in your experience of life and in the evolution of your soul. The decision is in your hands. Empower yourself to transform your life and to change your state to feel better, faster than you believe possible. Regardless of what you have or have not said or done—forgive yourself. Love *yourself as we love you—fully, completely, and unconditionally. Embrace your calling and master the exhilarating role of being your own best friend and coach, your own guru.*

If you would like to know more about Sandra and Daniel please visit www.TheBiskinds.com.

# APPRECIATION

Throughout our lives, we have been blessed to have an enormous number of people make profound contributions to who we have become—and are still becoming. *PEACE: Power Up Your Life* is the first of eight books in The CODEBREAKER PLATINUM Series. These books are a distillation of over thirty years of spiritual practice and study, powerful personal transformation experience, and our ongoing journey into becoming the best versions of ourselves.

With incredible gratitude to all the business and success mentors, coaches, transformational teachers and spiritual and mystical masters who have touched our lives with your books, your workshops and more importantly your presence, we say a truly heartfelt thank you. Thank you for your dedication in being the change we all seek and for sharing who you are with the world.

A special thank you to Jack Canfield for taking the time to read CODEBREAKER and give us your feedback on a very rough first draft. You told us a book is not ready for publication until it has been rewritten at least 6 times and encouraged us to get feedback from a minimum of 10 beta readers. Well, thanks to you, *CODEBREAKER: Discover The Password To Unlock The Best Version of You* was sent out to over 30 people whose feedback was instrumental in helping us rewrite it *more* than 6 times. Each chapter was written as a book in its own right, and feedback confirmed the importance of releasing them in the order that they appear in the Master Password.

With that in mind, to everyone who has already read and re-read the entire CODEBREAKER PLATINUM Series, we cannot thank you enough for your support, wisdom, and thoughtfulness in making these books better in every way. To all the beta readers, coaches, editors, and developmental editors who shared their ideas on how to simplify and make a deep subject easier to comprehend, we are eternally grateful.

Writing these books has been a rollercoaster ride of excitement and overwhelming gratitude to so many people. Very special thanks must go to Bill Bryant and Sandy Beamer who have devoted months to helping us in the rewriting process. Daily, they challenged us to give better explanations of concepts that were new to them or that they thought needed clarification or simplification. They wanted more examples and more stories to make the teaching more effective and memorable. Their lives have changed because of their total immersion into the information in each book. Can you imagine what a Godsend they were to us? After 30-plus committed years of spiritual transformation practice and study with the one transcendent desire to live an enlightened life, they helped us break down esoteric concepts that were natural and normal to us into bite-sized chunks to make it easier to digest and use in your everyday life.

Deepest thanks and endless love to all of our students and coaching and consulting clients whose dedication and courage to move beyond limiting blocks keeps us motivated to continually find better, faster, and more effective processes. You inspire us with your dedication and honor us with your trust.

Finally, we want to thank all our family, and our friends who have become family, for your continued support and love—without love the world would be a cold and unfriendly place instead of the warm, uplifting, and awesome place we are so grateful to experience. Thank you!

# WORKING WITH SANDRA AND DANIEL

EMPOWER   ENLIGHTEN   INSPIRE

Thank you for reading The CODEBREAKER PLATINUM Series. As personal transformation teachers, we invite you to continue to work with us on this open-ended journey, the evolution of our souls into enlightenment and wholeness.

Visit www.TheBiskinds.com for additional tools to continue your development and to see the many ways you can work with us.

# PEACE

*Fully connected to the light of my True Self,
Peace is my natural state.*

PLATINUM

# LOVE

*Unconditional love is my essence.*
*My purpose is to grow, evolve and have fun*
*expressing the love that I am.*

PLATINUM

# AWARENESS

*With awareness I intuitively see beyond ego mind stories and understand the big picture.*

PLATINUM

# TRUST

*I trust my True Self can discern the truth
in any situation which frees me from fear.*

PLATINUM

# INTEGRITY

*My Integrity never compromises the means
for an end so I am always whole and
trustworthy.*

PLATINUM

# NEUTRALITY

*Being neutral empowers me to realize freedom and wholeness and to have the life of my dreams.*

PLATINUM

# UNITY

*Integrating unity and oneness makes it natural for me to love and forgive everyone and everything.*

PLATINUM

# MINDFULNESS

*Mindfulness alerts me whenever I need to correct negative thoughts, feelings, and emotions to get neutral to be happy.*

PLATINUM

PLATINUM

19590291R00071

Made in the USA
San Bernardino, CA
04 March 2015